My Name is Charlotte

A Collection of Stories about People who Share my Name

By Allison Dearstyne

For my loving grandmother and friend, Charlotte Sacks

The name Charlotte is French and dates to the 1300s or earlier. It is the feminine form of the boy's name "Charlot" or "Charles" and it means "free man" or "petite." Since Charles has always been a name commonly given to royal baby boys in Europe, Charlotte became a popular name given to royal baby girls. There have been a lot of princesses, duchesses and queens named Charlotte! In E.B. White's novel *Charlotte's Web*, the character Charlotte is a friendly, witty spider who helps her pig friend Wilbur by writing messages about him while spinning her webs.

Did you know that many real heroes in history were named Charlotte? We will look at these seven extraordinary women who share your name:

Charlotte Mason
Charlotte Brontë
Charlotte Forten
Charlotte Lamberton
Charlotte E. Ray
Charlotte "Lotte" Auerbach
Charlotte "Lottie" Hawkins Brown

Charlotte Mason was a Welsh teacher and writer with a wonderful new mindset. She was born in 1842 in Wales. When she grew up, Charlotte Mason became a teacher and after ten years, she discovered a huge problem: The curriculum was super dry and boring.

Children memorized facts that they usually found meaningless and quickly forgot them after they passed their tests. Charlotte Mason had a vision for a more well-rounded and meaningful education. She wanted to educate a child's whole being, not just his or her mind.

How did she do this? She traded dry history textbooks for "living books" which were narratives written like an exciting story. Charlotte Mason wrote some "living books" on geography that her students found much more interesting than their old textbooks! Rather than having her students copy lists of words to work on handwriting and spelling, she chose short passages from classic books to inspire them. Charlotte Mason's students listened to works by composers and viewed masterpieces by great artists.

She was the first educator to recognize the merit in a new book, *Aids to Scouting*, by Robert Baden-Powell, and added it to her curriculum. This book was used to create the Boy Scouts and Girl Scouts. Her students sang, tied knots, hiked, spoke in different languages, read Shakespeare and the Bible. Through her lessons, Charlotte Mason emphasized the good habit of learning for the sake of learning, not just to pass a test.

Through the centuries, there have been many ridiculous ideas about educating children, but Charlotte Mason got it right! Make it your goal to learn for the joy of learning, just like Charlotte Mason did!

Charlotte Brontë was an English author who made a big impact in history! She was born in Yorkshire in 1816, the third of six children. Her father was a minister and her mother died tragically young, when Charlotte was only five years old. For the next three years, Charlotte's older sister Elizabeth took care of her and her siblings.

When Charlotte Brontë was eight, her father sent her and three of her sisters to a boarding school for daughters of ministers. The conditions of the school were dreadful; she would wake before sunrise, bathe in a basin of freezing, dirty water, eat a burnt porridge breakfast and suffer humiliating punishments for breaking the rules. At the end of the day, she and another girl shared a bed so small that they had to prop up their heads. Things got even worse when the two oldest sisters died during an outbreak of disease at the school. The Brontë sisters returned home, and Charlotte was never fully healthy again after her yearlong stay there.

At nine, Charlotte Brontë became a mother figure to her brother, Branwell, and her sisters, Emily and Anne. She took care of them and created imaginative stories for them. Together they wrote a saga about their make-believe kingdoms. When Charlotte Brontë told these happy stories, she unknowingly prepared all of them to be writers when they grew up!

As young women, the three Brontë sisters wrote poems, combined their works into one book and had it published. They used pseudonyms, or fake names, so they wouldn't reveal their identity. Why did they do this? Back in those days, women were not expected to be authors and the Brontë sisters knew that most people wouldn't want to read a book written by women. Their first book wasn't a bestseller, but later they each wrote novels under their male pseudonyms and achieved great success! The Brontë sisters revealed their identity after their books became popular.

Jane Eyre was Charlotte Brontë's first best-selling novel, and it is considered a classic today. She wrote it from the perspective of a child named Jane who attends a boarding school where the conditions were exactly like the school the Brontë sisters attended. In writing this, Charlotte Brontë shed light on important social issues of her day. Children were often ignored, and by writing a novel for adults from a child's point of view, she helped give them a voice.

As the novel continues, Jane grows up to be a plain governess who experiences heartbreak but sticks to her moral beliefs despite her trouble. Years later, Charlotte Brontë wrote the novel *Villette*, which is also considered a classic. Some the early readers criticized the main character, Lucy Snowe, for being unladylike but Charlotte Brontë was proud of her work.

After publishing these two novels, Charlotte Brontë married the love of her life, a poor man named Arthur Bell Nichols, against her father's will. This was another bold move for her day! She never regretted it, and they had a happy marriage.

We learn from Charlotte Brontë that we can use difficulties in our life to help others. Write about your experiences and you can be like talented Charlotte Brontë!

Charlotte Forten was a Black American writer and teacher of former slaves. She was born in 1837 in Pennsylvania to a wealthy and influential family. As a girl, she formed a habit of writing in a diary and kept this good habit into adulthood. Thanks to her diaries her life work was preserved, and we know a lot about her thanks to them!

As a young woman, she was an abolitionist, which was someone who worked to end slavery. Before the Civil War, she kept careful records of her daily work for this cause. When the war began, Charlotte Forten joined a movement committed to educating former slaves. She moved to South Carolina and wrote about her teaching experiences in her diaries. They reflect her intellect and her passion. Below are two of her diary entries and essays on teaching from her book *Life on the Sea Islands.*

"The first day of school was rather trying. Most of my children are very small, and consequently restless. But after some days of positive, though not severe, treatment, order was brought out of chaos. I never before saw children so eager to learn."

"The long, dark night of the Past, with all its sorrows and its fears, was forgotten; and for the Future — the eyes of these freed children see no clouds in it. It is full of sunlight, they think, and they trust in it, perfectly."

Being educated is a wonderful privilege. Think about all the things you learn in school and be thankful! Then you can be like dedicated Charlotte Forten!

Charlotte Lamberton was a deaf vaudeville and ballroom dancer. She was born in Idaho in 1917 and had an older brother, Charles. Both Charlotte and Charles were born deaf. When they were little, their mother homeschooled them and taught them how to lipread. Imagine being able to understand what people say by watching their mouths move but never hearing a sound! Later, Charlotte and Charles learned American Sign Language.

Wanting her to enjoy the same activities as other kids, Charlotte's mother put her in dance lessons when she was five. Right from the start, she excelled at dance. Charlotte Lamberton performed professionally in Hollywood when she was only 11, and sometimes her brother joined her onstage. By the time she was 14, she was known in shows as "The Exquisite Charlotte."

Charlotte's mother arranged for a two-week trial performing as a ballroom dancer in New York City. Everyone was so impressed by her that her tour stretched to be 28 weeks long, and she danced her way through the United States on a vaudeville tour! Vaudeville shows were variety shows. Charles and joined her, and the Lambertons made headlines around the country. Their dance routines were always stellar and right on beat.

People often asked Charlotte Lamberton how she danced to music she could not hear. They assumed she could feel the orchestra music through her feet. She said that she couldn't, but instead felt the music faintly pulsating through her whole body. She couldn't fully describe the sensation of feeling music to hearing people.

Too often, people with disabilities have been pushed to the margins and overlooked. But Charlotte Lamberton took centerstage and her talent amazed everyone! We learn from Charlotte Lamberton to never underestimate anyone because of a disability. Everyone you meet is filled with potential. Remember that and you can be like the exquisite Charlotte Lamberton!

Charlotte E. Ray was the first Black woman lawyer. She was born in 1850 in New York City, the youngest of three girls. Her father was a minister, abolitionist and owner of a newspaper. Her parents valued learning and provided their daughters with a proper education.

Little Charlotte moved with her family to Washington, D.C., where she and her sisters attended the only local school that allowed African American girls to be students. When she graduated, she taught at Howard University, a new historically Black college. She trained schoolteachers, but she really wanted to do something else with her career: practice law.

Two big obstacles stood in her way to becoming a lawyer: her race and her gender. But that didn't stop her! She applied to Howard University's Law School under the name "C.E. Ray" to disguise her gender, and her application was accepted. After it was discovered that she was a woman, officials at the university discouraged her from going through the program but allowed it, nevertheless. In 1872 she completed law school and became the first Black woman with a law degree in the United States!

The bar in Washington, D.C. removed the word "male" from its requirements, and she became the first woman admitted to it. Charlotte E. Ray opened her law office there and skillfully argued many cases, earning the respect of many of her coworkers. But unfortunately, most people did not want to hire a Black woman attorney. Unable to make a living as a lawyer, she moved back to New York to live with her sisters. She became a schoolteacher and fought for women's right to vote.

Although she did not fully reap the benefits of her hard work in her short career as a lawyer, she broke ground in a profession that had previously been reserved for White men. One day when you join the work force, be thankful for women like Charlotte E. Ray who helped pave the way for you!

Charlotte "Lotte" Auerbach was a Jewish Polish scientist who made an important discovery. She was born in 1899 in Breslau to Jewish parents who passed their love of chemistry on to her. She grew up in Germany and attended college there. As Lotte Auerbach grew, so did racism against Jews who lived in Germany. She quit school, discouraged by how badly she was treated because of her race.

Lotte Auerbach moved to Scotland, where things were much better for her, and she earned her Ph.D. there. She worked for her university doing research on gene mutations. Genes are tiny pieces that make up all living things. A gene mutation happens when some genes are naturally different from what is typical. Lotte Auerbach ran an experiment where she poisoned fruit flies and discovered that gene mutations can be changed with science!

Her research led to more discoveries by other scientists about genetics. Genetics is the study of all the characteristics we inherit from our parents. She wrote 91 scientific papers in her long, successful career. Scientists still use her research today!

When Lotte Auerbach retired, she became a champion activist, which is someone who works hard to make positive changes. She worked to rid the world of its most destructive weapons and helped bring down a racist system in South Africa called apartheid.

Lotte Auerbach was a hero who used her discoveries to help people. When you are sitting in your science class, pay close attention and you can be like smart Lotte Auerbach!

Charlotte "Lottie" Hawkins Brown was a Black American educator, author and founder of a school. She was born in 1883 in North Carolina and when she was seven, she moved to Massachusetts.

When she was a teenager, she earned money babysitting and committed herself to learning everything she could. Lottie Hawkins Brown recalled pushing a baby in a stroller while reading aloud from a Latin book when her life changed. Alice Freeman Palmer, the president of Wellesley College, overheard her reading and decided at that moment to become her mentor and help Lottie further her education.

When she grew up, Lottie Hawkins Brown moved back to North Carolina and taught in a small-town school. She loved teaching, but after her first year, the school didn't have enough money to operate and shut down. Determined to fix the problem, she raised money for the school and asked her mentor for financial aid.

Her campaigns were successful! The next year Lottie Hawkins Brown opened a new school in the same small town called Palmer Memorial Institute, which she named after her mentor. The school earned a reputation for excellence and expanded to include a junior college program. It was visited by some other great teachers of her day - Mary McLeod Bethune, Booker T. Washington and Eleanor Roosevelt.

By 1920, Lottie Hawkins Brown was a well-known public figure and in high demand as a speaker. She spoke on the value of racial equality, education, women's rights and even on social graces. She wrote several books on these topics too.

This is an excerpt from one of Lottie Hawkins Brown's books called *The Correct Thing to Do, to Say, to Wear* on how to act in a classroom:

1. Always greet the teacher when meeting for the first time, whether it be morning or not.

2. Be sure that you have everything you need - text, paper, pen, etc. Don't be a carpenter without tools.

3. When called on to recite, always make some sort of reply. Don't sit in the seat and say nothing. Don't even think too long. Valuable minutes are wasted thus.

4. When standing or sitting, hold yourself erect. Don't slouch. Talk clearly and sufficiently loud for everyone in the room to hear.

5. Don't make a habit of laughing at the mistakes of others. This often hinders a person from doing his best.

6. Don't deface property. Writing on or cutting into desks or chairs, writing and drawing in books, breaking the backs, or turning down the corners of pages of texts are evidences of poor training.

7. Make it your business to keep the room in order. Straighten the shades, keep the floor and desks free of waste paper, and erase the boards when they need it.

8. Don't Cheat. You will never learn by "copying" from your neighbor or from the book.

9. Do not argue with or contradict the teacher in class. If you think that she has made a mistake, wait until the hour is over and discuss it with her quietly at the desk.

10. Do not yell out the answers to questions; wait until you are called upon. The teacher will let you know when concert recitation is desired.

11. Don't mistake the classroom for a lunchroom or a bedroom.

She urged her students to act with kindness and dignity, believing this would speed up the long and hard process of earning equal rights. So, when you go to class, follow the rules of etiquette laid out by Lottie Hawkins Brown and you will be a great success!

This page is all about you!

_____ was born on

_____

As a baby, Charlotte _____

_____

As a little girl, Charlotte _____

_____

Charlotte is especially good at _____

_____

Charlotte is often described as _____

_____

Charlotte makes people laugh when she _____

_____

One day Charlotte would like to _____

_____

This page is for making a self-portrait. A self-portrait is a picture of you, drawn by you!

Bibliography

"A Student Remembers." *Charlotte Hawkins Brown Museum.* North Carolina Historic Sites. 6 Oct. 2015. Web. 7 Aug. 2018

Beale, Geoffrey. "Charlotte Auerbach." *Jewish Women: A Comprehensive Historical Encyclopedia.* Jewish Women's Archive. 1 Mar. 2009. Web. 11 Aug. 2018.

Cabiao, Howard. "Ray, Charlotte E." *Blackpast.org.* BlackPast. 8 Nov. 2010. Web. 12 Aug. 2018.

"Charles and Charlotte Lamberton Dancers Extraordinary 1936." newspapers.com/article/Detroit-free-press-charles-and-charlotte/11968677/ *Newspapers.com.* Detroit Free Press, 1 Nov. 1936. Web. 5 Jan. 2024

"Charlotte Hawkins Brown Biography." *The biography.com website.* A&E Television Networks. 26 Feb. 2015. Web. 7 Aug. 2018.

"Charlotte Forten Biography." *The biography.com website.* A&E Television Networks. 1 Apr. 2014. Web. 7 Aug. 2018.

McHugh, Catherine. "Who was Charlotte E. Ray?" *The biography.com website.* A&E Television Networks. 12 Jan. 2016. Web. 7 Aug. 2018.

"Only a Teacher: Charlotte Forten." *PBS.org.* WETA. Web. 10 Aug, 2018.

Tomkins, Joyce. "Charlotte Brontë." *Encyclopaedia Britannica.* Encyclopaedia Britannica, inc. 14 Apr. 2018. Web. 9 Aug. 2018.

"What is the Charlotte Mason Method?" *SimplyCharlotteMason.com.* Simply Charlotte Mason LLC. Web. 14 Aug. 2018.

Wikipedia contributors. "Charlotte (given name)." *Wikipedia, The Free Encyclopedia.* Wikipedia, The Free Encyclopedia, 7 Aug. 2018. Web. 14 Aug. 2018.

Wikipedia contributors. "Charlotte Brontë." *Wikipedia, The Free Encyclopedia.* Wikipedia, The Free Encyclopedia, 7 Aug. 2018. Web. 14 Aug. 2018.

Wikipedia contributors. "Charlotte Lamberton." *Wikipedia, The Free Encyclopedia.* Wikipedia, The Free Encyclopedia, 8 Sep. 2023. Web. 6 Jan. 2024.

Wikipedia contributors. "Charlotte Mason." *Wikipedia, The Free Encyclopedia.* Wikipedia, The Free Encyclopedia, 6 Aug. 2018. Web. 14 Aug. 2018.

www.ingramcontent.com/pod-product-compliance
Lightning Source LLC
Chambersburg PA
CBHW042110040426
42448CB00002B/219